A walk through the historic streets

Longer walk: about 2.5km (about 1.5ml); shorter walk: about 1.5km (less than 1m); both on level ground

This walk around the narrow and winding streets of Sandwich takes you through the historical heart of the town. The starting point is the Quay, which was once a lively harbour, not the quiet marina that it is today. During the Middle Ages the port of Sandwich was one of the busiest in the kingdom, with merchant ships from the Continent bringing wine, silk and spices and even pilgrims bound for St Thomas's shrine at Canterbury. Sandwich's merchants profited from this and built themselves great houses, some of which you will see as you walk around the town.

But the grand houses of Strand Street are only part of the picture. This walk will also take you through much less spectacular streets lined with two-storey dwellings with brick or plastered fronts. They often look as if they had been built in the 18th or 19th century, but many of them are fundamentally medieval, with timber-framed buildings hidden behind the later facades. These were mostly the homes of the mariners, craftsmen and artisans who made up the great majority of the townspeople.

We start at the Quay beside the river Stour (paying car park, and public conveniences)

Turn your back on the river and you will see a stone gateway built of flint and limestone. This is **Fisher Gate**, the earliest remains of the town's medieval defences (see Walls Walk for details). Walk through the gate and up to the top of Quay Lane where it is

crossed by **Upper Strand Street**. Looking left down the you will see opposite the (1), hiding a medieval fra

Cross from Quay Lane to **Fisher Street**, lined with two-storey houses. Many of their brick fronts disguise 15th-century timber buildings, of a rather modest type (3/4). Further on, The George and Dragon public house on the other side of the street (5) appears rather grander, but it was originally two small cottages, built just before 1600. Just beyond this, turn left into **Church**

as the starting point for civic processions. St Clement's is now Sandwich's only parish church.

It is open daily in the summer; guidebooks are available in English and five other languages.

Retrace your steps along Church Street St Clement until you come to a T-junction where you should turn left into **The Chain**, a short stretch of road which is lined with small 16th- and 17th-century houses, some with 19th-century shop fronts. When you reach King Street, look to your left along **Millwall Place**. At the far end you can see the town wall which was built in the 14th century across what was once the main southern route into and out of town (see Walls Walk for details).

Turn right along **King Street**, now one of the commercial hubs of Sandwich, with shops along much of its length. **Number 68** on the corner opposite the end of The Chain is a good example of a modern shop front on a 16th-century house. **Number 62, The Old Dutch House (7)**, was newly built in the 17th century with

Street St Clement and walk to the churchyard at the end. **St Clement's church** (6) was constructed about the year 1000 and was the first of Sandwich's three churches to be built in stone. Only a very few fragments of the earliest church survive, and its most prominent feature today is its magnificent 12th-century

tower. The church was founded on the highest point in the town, overlooking the harbour, and it would have been a landmark for shipping. It was always an important church: King Edward the Confessor attended mass there, and it was used as a royal court of law presided over by the king's bailiff. It also played a large part in the life of the town, as the place where the mayor was elected and

ornamental brickwork along the front (now painted). The windows and doorway were put in during the 18th century. Next to it, the **Sandwich Bookshop** was built as a shop in the 19th century. It preserves the original front and most of the internal layout of what was **Rose's Supply Store**. On the other side of the street, the building which is now numbered **27–29** was built in the very early 16th century as the rectory of St Peter's church. Its medieval origins can be seen in the jetty or overhang to the first floor. The mathematical tiles (imitating bricks) on its front face date from a renovation in the 18th century.

At the junction, bear right into **St Peter's Street**. On your left there is a fine 17th-century brick building now painted white (**8**). It is called **The Old Gaol** because it incorporates timbers from the medieval gaol which once stood on this site. Opposite is Holy Ghost Alley, now a lane used as a short cut through to the High Street, but in the late 14th century the timber doorway that frames the entrance led not into a lane but into a house now **Number 18** (**9**). Its

present appearance dates from the middle of the 17th century – a little later than the '1636' which you can see on the front at first-floor level.

The next point of interest is **St Peter's church** (**10**). This was a very large medieval church but in 1661 its tower collapsed, destroying the south aisle. The aisle was never rebuilt, but the wall was patched up to make the south side of the church, which overlooks a very small churchyard. Its central tower was restored in the late 17th century by descendants of the Strangers, refugees from the Low Countries who had come to Sandwich a hundred years earlier to escape from the religious persecution which they suffered in their homeland. They also restored the chapel at the south-east end of the church with a brick 'Dutch' gable, which you can see on the right.

Walk around the west end of the church, passing a fine 14th-century window, which stands isolated in the churchyard (**11**). It once lit the hall of the medieval St Thomas's Hospital, an almshouse founded in 1392 by Thomas Elys, a wealthy wine merchant. He was mayor and MP for Sandwich, and

lived in Harnet Street (see below **16**). The hospital stood between New Street and the Cattle Market until it was pulled down in the 1850s. It was then refounded in Moat Sole (see Walls Walk **15/16**).

Enter the church through the north porch. Even though it is now only two-thirds its original size, the church is very spacious, and in the 14th century the town's law courts were held in the wide north aisle (**12**). The fine tombs along the north wall commemorate town worthies who presided over the proceedings (**13**).

The church is no longer used for religious services and is looked after by the Churches Conservation Trust. It is open daily; a guidebook is on sale inside.

Turn left out of the churchyard into **Market Street**, called Fishmarket in the Middle Ages. When it was a market it had moveable stalls in the middle of the street and also permanent buildings around the edge. The earliest visible remains of these is a blocked window dating from about 1300 reset but still visible inside the **Public Library**. A late 18th-century drawing of **Numbers 4**, **6**, **8** and **10** shows what the buildings opposite it looked like before their jettied fronts were cut back and refaced. It is difficult to imagine that the row of buildings shown in (**15**) is the same one as in the drawing (**14/15**).

Walk along Market Street and The Butchery, where the town's butchers had their shops, towards Strand Street. On your left, the fine Georgian front of **Number 29 Harnet Street** (**16**) hides the house built for Thomas Elys in the 14th century.

At this point, those who wish to shorten the walk should turn right into Strand Street and walk along it back to the Quay. This street with its fine timber buildings is described on pages 8–9.

The longer walk continues down Harnet Street to Delf Street. On your right is a wall with part of a doorway and some finely knapped flints (17), once the garden wall of the Elys family home. Cross Delf Street and bear left towards **the Guildhall**

(18), in a pedestrian area which was once the Cattle Market. The Guildhall, Sandwich's Town Hall, was built in 1577–9 with a court room on the ground floor and a council chamber and treasury above. The building then underwent several modifications before reaching its present

appearance in 1973. The court room, which still contains much of its original layout and furniture, and the museum of town history are open to the public.

For information on opening hours and entry fees visit the Tourist Information Office on the north side of the building.

Diagonally opposite stands **No Name Shop** (19) in the short street that is now curiously called **No Name Street**. When the shop was built in the 15th century, it contained four tiny shops and a smithy for making small household articles. The smiths may have used water from the Delf in their work, even though it was the town's main source of drinking water throughout the Middle Ages (and even up to the late 19th century when the pump was installed). Not surprisingly, it was appallingly polluted.

A short walk along New Street brings you to **Number 20**, the home of one of Sandwich's most famous 18th-century residents (20). A tiny house dwarfed by a three-storey building next door, this is where Tom Paine lived and kept shop in 1759, long before he wrote The Rights of Man and achieved fame in America. When in Sandwich he was still plying his trade as a corset maker.

Retrace your steps, and opposite the Guildhall you will see on your right a very rare survival of early 20th-century public transport: a waiting room for passengers of the East Kent Road Car Company, built in 1921 (**21**). At the corner of Cattle Market and Delf

Street, Barclays Bank appears to be a modern building, but an elaborate timber doorway (now blocked up) with the town coat of arms, the date 1601 and initials WI above it show its early origins (**22a/b**).

Follow the Delf stream along the south side of **Delf Street**, which is a pleasant mixture of small medieval houses with later facades, 18th- to 19th-century houses, and a notable 20th-century

building in the form of the **Empire Cinema**, built in 1937 in classic Art Deco style (**23**). You will soon come to **Bowling Street** on your right, named after a bowling alley belonging to the medieval White Hart Inn in Strand Street (see below **31**).

Most of the houses in this part of town were built during the second half of the 16th century when the Strangers (refugees from the Low Countries, see page 3) brought prosperity back to Sandwich after a period of recession. Bowling Street is a good example of the mixed housing built then. There are small, flat-fronted, brick or plastered dwellings such as **Number 6–8**, which were originally semi-detached cottages for people of modest means (**24**). In contrast, **Number 7, Richborough House,** was a grand house built for a member of the town's elite (**25**).

Go round the corner of this house into **Vicarage Lane**, where there is a medieval stone doorway on your left, at **Number 3**, perhaps from the original vicarage. At the end of the street turn right into **Church Street St Mary**, one of the most charming streets in Sandwich (**26**). Late 16th- and early 17th-century

houses, **The King's Arms** public house and **St Mary's church** together form a picturesque grouping (**27**).

For much of the Middle Ages St Mary's was the finest church in Sandwich, it was the parish church for the west end of the town and had many prosperous merchants in its congregation. But its medieval interior was destroyed when the tower collapsed in 1668, and the building is now a concert hall rather than a church. It remains in the care of the Churches Conservation Trust, and is open daily. A guide book is on sale.

Standing with your back to the church, you will see a four-storey building, next to Gazen Salts car park and near the mouth of the Guestling stream which flows behind it. This is **Guestling Mill** (**28**), now an apartment block but built in the 19th century as the East Kent Brewery. It stands on the site of a 16th-century house in which Henry VIII is reputed to have stayed when it was owned by Sir Edward Ringley, the town bailiff. Another royal guest was Elizabeth I in 1572; after her visit one of the rooms was called 'the Queen's bedchamber'. The house then became known as The King's Lodging, but that is now the name of **46 Strand Street** (see below **31**).

Almost immediately next to Guestling Mill is **62 Strand Street** (**The Long House**), a timber-framed house (**29**) built around 1570 very likely for John Gilbert, a ship owner, member of the

Sandwich elite, and a typical parishioner of St Mary's church. Walk west along Strand Street, following the route that Queen Elizabeth I took from her accommodation in the King's Lodging to the newly established **Grammar (or Manwood) School**, so named

after its founder, Sir Roger Manwood (**30**). Built of pale yellow brick with decorative gables and chimneys and '1564' in ironwork on the front, it was a typical grammar school of that date with a large schoolroom

flanked by master's lodgings. It remained in use until 1858. In the 1890s it was refounded on a new site at the east end of town and the original building converted into private housing.

You have now reached the westernmost edge of the town, so return to the Quay by retracing your steps along Strand Street. On the return walk to the car park, you will pass **46 Strand Street** on your left-hand side (**31**). It was once called The Old House but is now known as **The King's Lodging.** Built in the 15th century as a merchant's house, it was enlarged in the 16th century to become the White Hart Inn, which had its bowling alley in Bowling Street opposite.

Walk on a little further and you will come to the junction of Strand Street and Harnet Street, where those opting for the shorter walk join with this one to follow what is in many respects the climax of the tour.

As you walk eastwards along Strand Street you will see one of the best medieval streets anywhere in Britain.

Numbers 37–41, 19–23, 13–15 and 11 on the south (right-hand) side of the street are particularly striking and were built in the 14th and early 15th centuries. At that time they stood on the bank of the river Stour, which flowed not where it does today but more or less along the line of the street where you are walking. The houses on the left-hand side of the street were not built until several centuries later, once the land along the riverbank had been consolidated.

Numbers 39 and 41 are among the best surviving medieval merchant houses in the whole of England (**32/33**). They both date from about 1334. Each has a great open hall and timber-framed fronts. The front wall of the first and second floors of **Number 39** still has the original timbers. Standing at the corner where Love Lane joins Strand Street you have another glimpse of medieval Sandwich. **Number 23**, beside you, had shops on its ground floor and an upper storey for storage; you can still see the shuttered opening where a hoist would have hauled heavy goods up into it (**back cover**).

A little further on, **Numbers 11–15** were used as an inn in the late 15th century (34). Behind them is one of the earliest buildings in the town. To see its ruinous remains turn right at the end of Number 11 into **Three King's Yard**, and it is on your right behind a modern garden wall (35).

It is unusual for Sandwich in being made of masonry, mainly local flint and brick imported from Flanders. Limestone from Normandy was used at the corners and around the elegant pointed windows which lit the merchant's private apartment on the first floor.

Retrace your steps into Strand Street and turn right to continue to the end of it where the Crispin Inn is your left, the Admiral Owen public house on your right, and the Bell Hotel in front of you (36). Turn right into **High Street** (37).

This is one of the widest streets in Sandwich, where a weekly market and annual fair (St Clement's Fair) were held. Its original medieval character can be seen in a few of the houses such as Numbers 40, 42 and 54, but the overall impression is of

18th-and 19th-century solidity. That is because around 1800 Sandwich's professional class chose to live in the High Street, and preferred to rebuild the houses in the style of the time. They often demolished everything old and built afresh, but some of the medieval houses were 'renewed' by being given new fronts.

Now turn back towards the river, and just before the Bell Hotel turn right into Upper Strand Street then left into Quay Lane, and so back to the car park.

A walk around the town walls

Longer walk: about 2.5km (about 1.5ml); shorter walk; about 1.5km (less than 1ml); both on level ground

Throughout much of the Middle Ages France and England were either at war or at best enjoying a precarious peace, and Sandwich was on the front line of England's defences. The legacy of all this is one of Sandwich's most fascinating, yet virtually unknown, monuments: its medieval defences.

Earth ramparts 1km long surround the historic core of the town on the landward side, and about 500m of stone wall run along all but the central stretch of the riverside. The four gates which guarded the entrances to the town from the east, south-east, south-west and south were demolished at the end of the 18th century because even then they were regarded as obstacles to traffic, but two stone gateways survive on the riverbank facing the harbour. The ramparts were landscaped in the 19th century to make a quiet park and gentle walk around the edge of town and it comes as a surprise to most people that what today is a peaceful open space was once fundamental to England's medieval war efforts.

We start at Guildhall Car Park (paying car park and free public conveniences).

The car park occupies an area of low-lying ground, little more than 2m above sea level, where a religious house for Carmelite friars (commonly known as White friars) was founded in the late 13th century.

Archaeological excavations have revealed the plan of the friars' medieval church and living quarters, but nothing remains above ground as all the buildings were demolished at the Dissolution of the Monasteries in 1538. When the friary was founded in 1268 there were no town walls and the built-up area finished just to the north of the friary land, along the line of the Delf stream which at that time marked the southern boundary of the town. The land which was given for the friary was wet and marshy and had to be drained before it could be built on. The drainage scheme involved building what are now called **The Rope Walk** and **The Butts**, two earth banks, with ditches on each side of them. Sometime early in the 14th century they were joined by **Mill Wall**, to become not just a drainage system but a defensive circuit.

Leave the car park by **Fellowship Walk** which leads to the **Rope Walk**. The name may come from the days when there were shipbuilding yards on the Quay in the early 19th century, but there is no other evidence to support this. In front of you is the water-filled moat, now a favourite haunt of fishermen (1).

Its ornamental appearance is deceptive for it was regarded as potentially defensible, not only in the Middle Ages but during the

English Civil War (1642–51), and even as recently as World War II when it was deepened as a tank trap .

Turn left, and walk along the Rope Walk until you reach New Street which was the site of **New Gate**, built before 1456 and demolished in 1782. New Gate guarded the entrance into Sandwich from the south-east. The Delf stream also flowed through the gateway in a man-made channel, as it still does here (2) and along New Street and Delf Street. It served not only as a water supply (and continued to do so until 1894) but also as Sandwich's only defence to the south until the ramparts were built.

When you cross New Street onto Mill Wall you will see that the rampart and moat to your right are very different from the bank and ditch of the Rope Walk. Firstly, the moat is dry, although when it was first dug it was filled with water. It was then open to the sea at its northern end by the Bulwark so that each high tide flooded it with salt water. The water reached as far as New Gate, where a brick wall served as a sea defence, and there was a constant battle to keep the fresh drinking water in the Delf pure. Finally a dam was built across the moat at Sandown Gate (**see below 5**), allowing just a trickle of water through a sluice, but the moat did not dry out completely until the early 19th century.

Immediately beside New Street the **Mill Wall** earth rampart slopes gradually upwards. After walking for about 100m you will reach the end of **Millwall Place**. It is now a cul-de-sac, but before the early 14th-century rampart was built, Millwall Place was a through route, the continuation of the main road from Worth, Deal and Dover. Even though the road was blocked in the early 14th century, the original route is still a footpath connecting Millwall Place with modern housing outside the town walls.

On the left there is a good view of the tower of the parish church of St Clement. Founded over a thousand years ago, the church stands on what passes for high ground in Sandwich. Its tower must have been visible for miles out at sea, a useful landmark for ships coming into the harbour.

After a further 100m you will reach another right of way, leading from Knightrider Street towards the railway station. As was the case with Millwall Place, **Knightrider Street** became a cul-de-sac when the rampart cut across a branch of the road from Worth. Mill Wall also changes in alignment and character here, becoming very much higher and with steeply sloping sides. The corner is the highest point in Sandwich, and the place where the windmills that give the rampart its name stood as early as the 15th century (3). The last surviving mill burnt down in 1895.

Walk along top of the high stretch of Mill Wall (4). On your right, but usually obscured by trees, is **Castle Field**, the site of Sandwich's royal castle which was built in the 13th century and fell out of use during the reign of Henry VIII, when it was dismantled.

A tower, its last remaining feature, was removed in 1881. Today there is nothing left of the castle except a field name, but archaeological finds and historical documents give us some idea of what it looked like and why it was built there, apparently standing apart from the town. Excavations have shown that when the castle was built it was not outside the town, and only became cut off from it when Mill Wall was laid out about a hundred years after the castle was founded.

The separation was so complete that today most people who live in Sandwich are unaware that their town ever had a castle. Yet for more than a century Sandwich was crucial to the defence of the realm and the castle played a vital part in the war effort against France, particularly during the Hundred Years' War (1337–1443).

That was when most money was spent by the Crown in making the castle fit for its role as the embarkation point for kings and their armies. Edward III, Henry IV and Henry VI passed through

Sandwich on their way to or from France. While waiting for their ships, thousands of troops and their horses camped out in the fields around the castle, sometimes for months. The townsfolk must have been relieved to have Mill Wall as a barrier between them and a potentially riotous army.

Leave what is now a peaceful pasture and walk along Mill Wall until you reach Sandown Road, which is the site of **Sandown Gate**. The gate was demolished in 1782 but 18th-century pictures give us some idea what it looked like just before that (5).

Archaeological excavations have also unearthed some remains, including some courses of brick from the south-east tower. The feature is now very overgrown but can be seen on the slope of the ditch just below the level of the road.

Cross to the other side of Sandown Road and go through the gate on your left into the park beside **the Bulwark** (6). It is difficult to imagine that this grassy area was once the harbour for the castle, where ocean-going ships were

loaded with men and horses, and set off for France. Timbers from a merchant ship that sank here in the 14th century were found in the 1970s and others may remain to be discovered.

The Bulwark was built as an artillery fortress in 1451. It took up the north-east corner of the town, was surrounded by thick walls of earth with brick and stone facings that are still there, and was armed with a variety of 'great guns' from the arsenal which was kept in the body of the fort. The tidal waters of the river Stour and Sandown Creek filled the moat in front of it. The Bulwark was intended as Sandwich's main defence against possible attack from the sea and it was put to the test by a French raid in 1457. The fort may have borne the brunt of the brief but deadly attack, in which the mayor of Sandwich was killed, for it seems to have been damaged quite badly. Even ten years later it was still being repaired. This is in contrast to the castle, which may have escaped more lightly. The only remains of the fort are the walls on the east and north sides. When you walk westwards beside the north wall you will see that the river is 50m or more to your right, but in the 15th century the riverbank was much closer to the wall, lined with wooden quays, and with the mouth of Sandown Creek open to ocean-going vessels.

All the buildings inside the Bulwark had been demolished by the 18th century, and even archaeological traces must have been removed by recent landscaping. The area of the Bulwark now belongs to **The Salutation**, a mansion designed by Edwin Lutyens in 1911 with a garden originally laid out by Gertrude Jekyll.

The newly restored 'Secret Gardens of Sandwich' are open to the public (entry fee). Access is from The Quay or Knightrider Street.

Continue walking with the river on your right. Some of the stones in the walls of the houses at the corner of The Quay and Knightrider Street probably come from the town wall (**7**) which from here to The Barbican was made of stone, not earth. The wall itself is visible further on.

Cross the end of a narrow alley to **The Keep**. Until recently this was called 'The Round House' and it had a curved extension on its north side fronting the quay. Tradition has it that the upper room once housed the mechanism for a chain (known as a boom) which could be slung across the river to defend the harbour.

Continue walking westwards until you reach **Fisher Gate** (**8**). The lower two storeys were built in flint and limestone in the late 14th century. The upper part, of yellow brick with a diamond-shaped decoration was added in about 1500 and the present gable above it was built in 1581 (this date is on the plaque in the apex of the gable, but is now indecipherable).

The gate was built to guard one entrance into the town from the harbour. Its central passage was defended by doors and a portcullis (you can still see the slot for it), and there was a wharf on the riverbank in front of it. A yellow-brick meeting hall was built on the gate's west side in 1869 and its north face suffered unsympathetic restoration in the 1990s.

The **town wall** can be traced for about 100m further west, until Quay Lane and the 19th-century Bell Hotel break its line. The upper part of the wall, where there is a patchwork effect of many shades of brown, has been repaired many times but below that you can see some courses of large stone blocks which are remains of the original wall (**9**). The stone is ragstone, quarried near Folkestone and shipped to Sandwich in the 15th century. The riverside here was the quay belonging to the town (known as the Town Quay or Common Quay). Most of the rest of the riverbank was lined with private wharfs belonging to individual merchants.

Walk along past the Bell Hotel and cross the road to **The Barbican** (**10**). There has been a gate on or near this site since 1300, although throughout the Middle Ages it was known as Davis Gate or Daveygate. By 1776 its name had been changed to the Barbican for no very good reason, but that is what it is called today.

Recent research has shown that, contrary to local legend, the present gatehouse was built in 1467–70 (during the reign of Edward IV) not in 1538 (towards the end of Henry VIII's reign). The chequerwork decoration of alternating squares of flint and limestone makes it one of the most spectacular gates in any small town in England, and suggests that Davis Gate was put up partly as a status symbol, as a welcome but also a warning to those who came to Sandwich by sea. It was built at a cost of almost £200, a great sum in those days, but as it was founded on wooden piles sunk into the river bed it seems not to have been very stable, and a great deal more money needed to be spent on it over the next hundred years.

Once you walk through the gateway you are inside the medieval walled town. Turn right into **Strand Street**, with the **Crispin Inn** to your right and the **Admiral Owen** public house to your left. Both are 15th-century in date and full of character. This was the mercantile centre of the medieval town, and still has grand timber-framed buildings along its south side (on your left).

Until about 1400 there was no proper street between the houses and the river, and each house had its own wharf in front of it, probably surrounded by walls or fences. Between these were public rights of way to the waterfront, three of which survive as the lanes called **Ives Gate**, **St Mary Gate** and **Pillory Gate**. Gates at their riverbank end could be locked and safeguarded at night or in times of danger, but they can have contributed little to the defence of the town. Nothing remains of them except their names. Details of the Strand Street buildings can be found in the Historic Streets walk.

If you wish to shorten this walk, the corner of The Butchery is a good place to stop. The Guildhall car park can be reached by following The Butchery and Market Street, then crossing to No Name Street and past the Guildhall (for details of the buildings that you will pass, see the Historic Streets Walk).

The longer route

The tour of the full circuit of the walls continues along Strand Street. Archaeology has shown that there was no town wall along the river bank from The Barbican as far as Guestling Mill. This is not surprising as most medieval ports left their quaysides undefended. In Sandwich, short stretches of stone wall survive west of Gazen Salts car park. As they are in the back gardens of private houses (11) they are not accessible, but you may catch a glimpse of them if you go along Guestling Walk which runs from the Gazen Salts car park to the west end of Strand Street.

Continue along Strand Street, passing the old Manwood School

on your left and crossing the Dolf which flows under the road. Near here was the site of **Canterbury Gate** (12). There is nothing left of the gatehouse, but until it was demolished in 1785 it stood at the western entrance to the town, straddling the high road from Canterbury. Judging from an engraving and a few stones from one of its towers, it was a small version of the West Gate at Canterbury (13). A pivot stone for a door post, which may have come from the gate, forms part of the collections in the 1760 smock mill (originally known as Canterbury Gate mill) that is the centrepiece of the **White Mill Rural Heritage Centre**, about 500m along Ash Road (entry fee).

Just beyond the Delf you will see a public footpath sign to **The Butts**. This is the longest stretch of rampart, running from Strand Street to Moat Sole and was originally intended to drain the land behind it as far as the Delf. In the Middle Ages the flat land in front of the rampart was called 'the butts' as it was used for archery practice. The land is now The Butts Recreation Ground and the rampart also bears the name (14). As you walk along The Butts try to imagine its being defended by cannon on gun emplacements that were built into the rampart in 1643 when the town refurbished its defences early in the Civil War. One of the earthworks remains, but is usually so overgrown that it is very difficult to spot.

When you reach Moat Sole you are at the site of Woodnesborough Gate. On your left you will see **St Thomas's Hospital (15/16)**. This is an almshouse which was moved here in 1857–8 when the medieval hospital of the same name was closed down (see also Streets Walk).

Cross the road to rejoin The Rope Walk. After 100m you will see the steps to Fellowship Walk and Guildhall Car Park on your left.

Acknowledgements

The author is very grateful to Lesley Orson for walking along the routes, and to English Heritage (EH.NMR), Giles Clarke (GC), Ray Harlow (SGA), Keith Parfitt (KP) and Sarah Pearson (SP) for supplying the photographs as credited below. Many thanks also to John Hills who drew the maps and Allan Adams (ATA) who drew the houses. Members of the Sandwich Heritage Group kindly commented on the text, but any mistakes are the responsibility of the author.

Maps reproduced by permission of Ordnance Survey on behalf of HMSO. © Crown copyright 2011. All rights reserved. Licence number 100046522

Covers: EH.NMR; GC, ATA

Streets walk
EH.NMR: 4, 9, 11, 19, 22a, 22b, 23, 25, 27, 30–34, 36
GC: 6, 10, 12, 13, 15, 16, 17, 20, 21, 24, 26, 28, 29

Walls walk
EH.NMR: 9, 10, 15; SGA: 3; KP: 8, 11; SP: 13

Antiquarian engravings are taken from W. Boys, *Collections for an History of Sandwich*, (1792), and H. W. Rolfe, *The Publications of the Antiquarian Etching Club 3*, (1852)

© Helen Clarke 2011

ISBN 978-1-84217-456-2

A CIP record for this book is available from the British Library

This book is available direct from Oxbow Books, Oxford, UK
(Phone: 01865-241249; Fax: 01865-794449)

The David Brown Book Company, PO Box 511, Oakville, CT 06779, USA
(Phone: 860-945-9329; Fax: 860-945-9468)

or from our website: www.oxbowbooks.com

Designed by Val Lamb
Printed in Great Britain by Information Press, Eynsham, Oxfordshire